Phantom

Limbz

(alternating
host
and

guest)

ISBN-13: 978-0692472187

Phantom Limbz

(alternating host and guest)

poetry and prose

by

Kevin M Sheetz

CONTENTS

—

untitled 1

Because of astrologers
the rain falls
on brass bosoms

Because of snakes
the rake glides
effortlessly

Because of the
illicit formula
ghosts are set on fire

The nightingale
would free its head
from its chain
and soak the lungs of the
sky
in vinegar

for nine pennies or more
again

Rock

the pale remainder
of the clipped and pert print
suction cup
oily
spread
fanning itself with leaves
gizzard trails
bellowing faraway laundromat
in the mire of dreams betide
side by sidle long and forth
fur hearing too bold
for a rumored manure field
bleeding like a frown a cloud
a clown emptying useless pores
forsaken girdle
moisten my facet
my lubrication paralyzing
and smelling often doldrums
human ditty
a blank squirt acres of desert housing systems
props behind the folded legs
and dire soiling
suckling sucking
the feverish nose
freckled and spiraling like a lioness
in the park
bedtimes

In Exchange for Delight

it is not only
a head in
the sand it yields
cacophonous salutations
undermining the twining fish holes
wingspan
you have fallen
get up
what are you doing
the lagging umbrella
cannot pale toward
the tripod inoculation
on its own
the lights' flight
places little
shells on
all the outlines
in
the vicinity
of precincts
succinct
like a
node
a bottomless boat
would never cherish
the flexing stringiness
stingy
it slides along

on the rest of vision
a humped mass
cowering in the corner
meat market
general
it couldn't touch it
too tenderly
to bring in the
morsels
for shivering upscale
mercenaries
plough unripe tires
under the
amber
your place of work
surrendering
hospitals to the
ribbed horses
in handcuffs
marketing the
bulletin
smoldering
meat particle
slinging machine guns
likes cantankerous
bananas
charge
no charge

The Betrothal

no more will I lean
my elephant
against the banister
no more
proffer my whale
to the glacial witness
sitting crooning
like eyes
in their nests
keys in
their pod
trembling
withstanding
the incorrigible wastes
that beckon like a mirage
glittering goods and services
in an array
feeling neither one way
or another
pushing through blind and empty
resting calloused hands
on mountain peaks
lethargy of the mind
can only give rise
to the image
of a little kitten

in the knoll
the will
swollen and hollow
lolling about like a ship in port
but the captain is
drunk and sleeping
and the crew
has frozen
sand burst

Glowing Glowing Lamb

mismatched eels I break one
hand
two three
four hand
hand hand
five letter-opening hands
bar lender
baroque daily
the latch the latch
one nine one hunt thoroughly
bend at noon
diaper hand leaning mouth
bank malleable tetrahedron collider
put put
put milk
put hand hankering
hunkering blown tubing deified defiler
with wrist
watch
sodden meld it's too tight
bright clue
none nun none homely
chimerical sing
to never year
wrapping up early iceberg floe

fallopian gangway walks alone
a hairy hatcher
midst
jewelry clones
clone clothes
cloth clone funeral
slit
slit slit

Sole Soul

The bare hands and
feet
in the corner
leaned up
against the wall

a person inside of
a person
with yet another
person
inside still

sometimes I think
that perhaps my soul
has its own soul
within it
and perhaps
I am someone's soul
and this world is their
body
that there is a person
on the outside
and then I think
to whom does this endless
procession of souls
belong?

am I the soul
within my soul?
all of this
cannot be mine
I wouldn't want it
anyway

thinking is like
a rickety rope ladder
trembling up and
up
into nowhere
it is better to climb down
and come back
home

where everything is peaceful
and still
these noises are just silence
stretching its hind legs

Sleeping On It

delusions arise
with the self
the self
is
delusion
above, a mourning dove
turning about
in midair

the old body was delusional
the new body functions
quite properly
it's astounding
it's available
it's mesmerizing
I can watch it for hours
the hours
which drip by
unknown
echoes resounding
but to fall on
no ears

when decisions unfurl
vaguely along the backdrop
I stand behind

I can be very large
I can be much smaller
it drifts by like a fragrance
catching one's nose

and when I wake up
there will be no more dreaming

No Words

It is not the world
that disturbs you
it is your mind
that disturbs you

one hundred thousand thoughts arise
but if you don't hold on to them
it's as if they're not even there

the mind suddenly unsheathed from thought
and the world is open to you

you can see your self

you can see your self
in everything
and everything
in your self

until there is not a thing
anywhere
not even
your self

Wind Rover, Dawn Rover

a prolific
horse mutilator
by seashore lined seasons
that are side by side
afore the lamp and moon
the horoscopes
put a bricolage there
twice nape of the neck
mice from the wreaths
of compilation
fueling enough
tilted companions under long fire
mortar
execute the dreams
tightly aligned
on the faded summer gasses
whose pouter
is lecherous abysmal felicity
meowing like some day's fat
tuna disc
sap-leaking separation
swift tonsil subjected out
lawful brain
ivory
creepers prosthetic desiccation
moon manure

mule manure
femur graciously manure
plasticity maturation above the
known bologna infiltration
upper stale traitorous aiding
insular porcelain scales
topped cleft oft sighting
the white
crumpers
adorned specifically
tubular viscous train
liner tiling tilling future cobalt hens obligated
scapes
these clumps
are outmode
talcum
mopish ear loaminess

ghvd231 fcfghvbj g8g54gc
part one

the late pretender
has an inkling
a rhino at first
then perhaps a small
desk in the corner
gloom
a child's balloon
traces light in the sky
open air molecules
cluttered like ants
in the ashtray
of a sphinx
purposes have become
quite forgoing
extinct
it goes with a loud popping
taken for something else
by our plaid anxiety footprints

our purple selves
our purple cells
prison self
clowning maliciously
prism cells
cellulose

armament
fortuitously
benighted
brawn

you're too loose
straighten up
there isn't a laughing
matter
it's the craving blotter
sinister teeter-totter
masquerading
as the dreams of us
which we give such endowment

spiderwebs
flowering over
the porcelain
platypus
they're standing in line together
with the rats and hat pricks
stinking toothache
of the eyes and blinking mind
dance
twirling idiot foam
splashing the tractors
out of reach
in the spiel
unspooling ruthlessly
twisted

mind frame
squeeze dark
on its platter death desk

the chains do chafe
everyone knows it
in their toes
in their throes
to and fro
bewildered pedestrian
having nothing to do
with anything
your way
untied
and glittering
spitting
deaf and crouched

ghvd231 fcfghvbj g8g54gc
part two

I cannot believe there was
yesterday
memory is
superstition
fabrication
forced upon us
by an authority
that isn't there either
the totems are hollow
the braying of crickets is heard
from within
bouncing off the moon-shape
stuck eternally in our vision
our mistaken vision
our created vision
made by no one
piles of dampening material
illicitly spread
lulling the drifting plains
to their knees
the dream of bees
unattained
darling flight
fruit in the hand
long hands drawn

uptight sitter
lachrymose banister

the big lick:
1) the judgement of other people
validates you
2) the judgement of other people
is almost always biased/corrupted

like an erupted volcano
tramp
licking moon dust
cotton tongue
benign up the cactus
proliferating on the tip
of each needle
the sand of a thousand Ganges

oh the dawn
mewling cheddar
foraging through
the complimentary
bladder
oozing cows at
every turn
the tables
blitz alone
rigor of a deer
jaunting left right
furrowing the steel cables

into positive
endorsements
open lantern
burgle lenses
attraction discreet flapping
amounts to pleasure
fully

hermetic
growth hormone
put it in a mouth
smog mouth
at the base of those
feelings
little wind wagons on the
branch
in stilettoed silhouette
worms and
cares
hairs
the fair kid mane
manger girth
trundling lucite

the corpse bound
in a single inward
strangulation
popping fizzing a witch's
ditch
poison sandals

laced with
carry on contrition
triton
if you asketh nine
regurgitated
method
blue brute
coat of harms
to another

hay bale sailor
siphon into my
vicinity
the hail flopping out
of your cat
discourages the quantity
of movie-goers
moving clovers
they're leaning
screen upon scream
dancer upon foot
dweller anon the
hanging wraith
that may loot like
somehow one's nose
turns off

fraying temperament
train whistle see it coming
undo the slopes
mistakes maximally
exerted
perturbed influence

The Mine of Secrets

buns and hoses
stepladder my nanny
one goes in one goes out
if I wish to
accompany horses
everywhere
it's got to start somewhere
inching abreast the pike
hat in my dogshit ass
fleas of perfume
wanker to the coven
of spoils
you inbred luminosity
biting the breasts
out before the turnpike
with black translucent angels
in parentheses
no one's looking
it hugs the iguana tightly
as they float through the
cornstalks
clamoring the mule deer
who put a diamond hand
down up the throat
clutches discreetly
the larynx

together
fanny bender
dilapidated toes in the tulips
stinking horse ovum
breathing in my pride
by its twinkling
dust eyes turn to smiles
molten snowman
you are concrete
of the stone held in
the bird's grasp
not the ribbon bird
not the soluble inclination
never wear the fervently
discarded hair
to bed
you drawer
yon winter harvest folds
sanguinely
demur
itched piles of rubble
withholding the claimants
of accredited
exposure
mule rhino the muddy
fingers lapse
decoding your musk
your mollusk
dismay
dramatic other acquaintance

distant user
beguile me
outside my head
the passageway
lit by intestines billowing
favorably
pluck me right there
right in my salamander

It Is Always Changing

the ground is littered
with leaves
that are not there

fallen from every tree

they are insects
very small
sitting weightlessly
on a
bubble that quivers
shimmering
with ecstasy

the thin wire
stretched horizontally
where invisible smiles hang
like fish

and the empty wall
elaborate costumes

God Looks Like Everything

this or that
in the rain

little pebbles of water
crouch like eagles
on the skin
of emptiness

effort or effort
sliding in the mud

once I have new teeth
everything will get better
it takes time
and time gets older
like a dog
a dog should have three wings
and so should flowers

my occasions in a suitcase
with my engagements
the pennies escape from my purse
to play with the cats
and the cats go inside
because it's raining
or snowing
I am layered
in snow

when there are
enough
flowers
the table has different shoes
just in time

trying forever
to match my heartbeat
with God's
in the corner of the room
there are two statues
made of ice
it's mother father
angels of memory
and precious metals
the marinade of insects
will blow their flugelhorn
when the lamps
are hung high in the evening
eclipsing the sun and moon
the purr of light
masking all
sound

beneath folded wings
shoes
snow
my God, my everything

HELP

what is it
that sings the song
of myself

and how will it end
echoing down
the long corridor
rippling
against nothing

emanating like light
dashed apple made
of light
consumed by the
eye
held up
against the sky

the rain will wash it away

maybe what afflicts you
also afflicts me
then so what?
so be it

maybe there is something

the rain can't wash away
but
I'm only guessing

it may not be like this
at all

I can't help it
I'm trying
I'm unarmed
help me
I'm not in control
of my perceptions

before the impenetrable glaze
I'm waving my hands
above my head
in surrender
defeat

there is no you
just us
there is no us
just you

Ignorance / Concentration / Privacy

the soothing light
while I'm looking away
drawn here and there
with no weight
the things that are around me
sit guilty
stripped of the masks
I hung on them
I'm hiding behind every object
but I'm not there
I'm hiding behind my mind
but I'm not there
just light

no-mind
all at once
at the fore
breathing
blinking

that which I wait for
long for
strive for
non-attainment

seamless

letting in
giving out
effortless

forgetting

(what is) the self
that is neither
affirmed nor denied
that neither
affirms nor denies

when you are transparent
you gain entrance
the world passes through you
like a gentle breeze

the chiming of a bell
stirred by wind
reaches to the center
it is waiting for you

The Accumulating Pile of Dust

the world is very small
         like a
    hummingbird
       flitting nudity through
            space
       forever seeking out the nectar
       of the sun

          the world is
          very small
          like a hummingbird flitting
nudity through space forever
    seeking out the
       nectar of the sun

        the world is very
    small like
          a hummingbird flitting
          nudity through space
forever seeking
       out the nectar of the sun

The Evening Symphony

birth birth
fortunate birth
a turtle is stepped
on by a giraffe
its broken shell
resembles my heart
lapidary fungus
each of its chambers
is a different choir
when there is birth
there is an eagle in
the upper left chamber
its calcified beak
scratches the iron bars
that extend into the
reflection of a
cloud on the sea
a machine is growing there
it's birth
miraculous birth
trimming the hedges
birthright
around a transparent
brain
with two ears attached
they flutter in the wind

they trample aphids underfoot
the etching of a
lizard in stone
has unbearable flatulence
and the fidgety colors in the
sky double over

Flute Prowess

murmuring
to great effect
the animal
of indeterminate volume
squarely focused
ornamented by the precocious
frost
a great gathering unfolds
hurtling asteroid
of senses
pulsing
by the stream
where a child sits
on a lily pad
the monotonous brushes
tug at
cold fur
a sparkling thermometer
in broad daylight
legs splayed
a canopy

Marrow We

the time field
is indeed
malformed
it starts in the erect
stone penis
and ends in the vaporous
space-mists of the vagina
it begins on the bookcase
and finds completion in the
microwave
macrocosms
the fossilized tracts
of pleasure booger
a grasshopper sheds
its birdbath into the
faucet
the economy starts
and is suspended
sidelong the
foreign tastes

death belongs to yesterday
today it is not here
it was never anywhere
time is only seen from behind
galloping away into the distance
the tumult of its wings

gives it the illusion of
transparency

see through to the other side

we cling like ticks
underneath its scales
water or air
depends
time is moldy
let's get a new one
it's simply picking
one or another
there's nothing to it
at all
cost
worth
companionship
steamship
formidable penguin
to port
and farther
away
clinking our eyelids together
shrill burst
down to the very center
of bones
below bones
it blows

Knock

the middle of
the table
hatched
a bright idea
a steam-powered
fingernail to
inch along
at its disclosure
until it cracks the clay winter
the pieces will abscond with
the tote
a prestigious gristle
to muck about
the lame
the shellfish brine of
brain supplicants
forging a stouter season
that of quintuplets
octopus barefeet trifling the tops of roses
petrified gloaming is
too facile unraveling dumbwaiter

untitled 2

artificial puttering around
                    butterfly
             hieroglyphic fluttering by
             lean tilted glance sword
                    release from its bonds
the isotopic platoon of memorials
                    bumbling
                    fly

Newt Glyphs

it all began with the Incas
climbing out of the doorstops
in Azerbaijan
it's all been said before
and written
they tell you
every stack of hay
and they've got beakers
full of them
so full of themselves

those abridged
steel pelicans
don't quite seem
particularly interesting
no investment
hot flapjack sacrament
wing your turn
priority malignancy

the blesséd relieving
crooked today pointing at noon
uninhabitable
they indicated crossly
rubbing it tight
I agree it is more

to lose
again
the storied hive
market
private mahogany
the privy unattained
to loosen its belongings
altogether a funeral swell
last attaching
circle around a waist
in a horn smoothly
the blessing hour of arraignment

So Many Things To Remember,
So Many Things I Can't Forget

I love that golden hole
when it wags and thistles
in the side of a mountain
marquee
pass your fervor
around this drought
sitting like a duck in its hands
piles of laughter
and porous

to the dark sex
biting the treetops
its laughter is very becoming
like ant milk
that foams as it whistles
and skirts the
hitherto predisposed nationality
of the ancillary pupa
nonchalantly rubbing its
whiskers
against a telephone mule
a flag pole
covers the red onions
with its
precision

and before it is a formlessness
very bloated
calling out to
the unresponsive brick
the shade of dreams
clueless
made of mud
made of the sweet piccolo
toot toot toot
it resounds
like a fire hydrant
covered in grass

Not Listening

there are so many balms!
there are so many elixirs!
which is the right one
for me?

why should I be opposed
to the idea
that there are things
in the world?

yet it seems
that they are not
it
that they are not where
it is

why must I have some
connection
with it?
but my separation is as imagined
as my
intimacy

sometimes I feel the
spirit leaping and dancing
within me

and sometimes not
lying cold like ashes
as if it were not there

I am the wavering
midpoint
between two
actualities I can
never grasp

O! to pause and rest
if only for a moment

though
this coming and going
isn't so bad
it appears to be the only thing there is

Cold Moment

it has dropped its glasses
onto the floor
where there are grasshoppers
around the rim
of the moon

spreading the ointment
so that it fills
the cracks in the landscape
the even surface of the sky
full of holes
full of mice

beyond
at the end of flowers
petals
close
around glistening tadpoles

imprisoned by faces
where there are none

Light from the Lighthouse

imbued
with the finest delicacies
    the starfish
        gloats ponderously
           along the curtains
           of the
           sea

           star

Mottle Mother Runner

let the hosts
cauterize their
children
like the breadcrumbs
of caterpillars
grazing o'er the moon
of prominent fuel

to assault the fabric glacier
it takes robed hands
it balances globed feet

it follows the
monotonous fur torpedoes

it does not listen
it does not glisten
it does not listen or glisten
to the shrill death-birds
following through
a suit of armor

Stalled

if it's all vomit
then beg my pardon
earnestly straying
monotony foothold of
the mind bind
metal grind together
in harmony
the ghouls
of tranquility
in foolish pools
old days
and tomorrow again
today
it was yesterday
at the store
schlepping into it twice
like a darn fat
swallowing the bungee cord
believably member

do you see
that all walls
are the same wall
every wall
is one wall
and we continuously put it up

every day
without realizing it
we mend and fix
and strengthen the wall
all the while
in innermost privacy
believing that we're doing
what we want
attending to our own affairs
of great impotence
importance

when you're in the meadow
don't gloat, please

Along Time

sun hero cactus hero
vast healer
emblazoned on the
stiff
horizon
jutting like
mountain peaks
brilliant propagation
of white
needles
the finger is
pricked like a
chicken and
wind is blown
through the sun's
snout
and whispers gently
to the cactus
needles:
"I'm so big
I'm the roundness
of an actual
square
the rotundity
of all endeavors"

the tongue is pricked
and a spleen of
blood
hesitantly reflects
the sun's
outline
in the sand

Rocking Chair Guardian

Catfish swimming
at the break
of dawn
caught in the hollow eye
of the old oak
tree

wood drawn
from its trunk
was carved into a perfect
sphere balanced
luxuriously
on the tip of a
pyramid

oh so long
ago

the infinite child
mewling
the cosmic crickets
chirping
successfully

Libation

I can hear the heavens
barking
just past the door
with each cough
I gather strength
for the winter
pulling down the blinds
I witness
a cactus who is pulling
on its wagon
an emerald bull
reared up on its hind
legs
in an expression
of attack
and my eyelashes
fall to the floor
like soldiers

the crying stems

jagged seclusion
big clicking

the armadillo sprouts
thousands of legs

and wings
its face honking
with sagacity
militant insects
pouring gasoline
over the cities
as if to douse
them

to the
bombs
going off
I offer
my hand
underneath
the fingernails
are spirits
a thousand ears
lined up in a row
into each one I insert
something special

Eater

the victim's body
chicken body
the victim's body
chicken body
the victims' body
chicken boy
chicken boy
give me the toy
give me the
toy
give
me
the
toy
give me
the
soy

the glass smoke
of an erect
cigarette
fills the lungs and stomach
like water
being poured into
a charming vase
full of flowers

at the center
is a little mouse head
it's winking

put the water in your molecule
it is raining
seeds of all different ports

Bungled

antiseptic thoughts
burrowing like bananas
the inward furrowing brow
digging through
the depths
to reach the
core
always out of reach

rushing torrent
of birds
amidst the
daemonic croaking

the crow man
tufts of coral reef
sticking in his gums
hidden by
a silver beak

it's too hard to tell
at this length

the certain animals
which bend and sway
like tall grasses

hold no ground
above their tinted
tusks
their tilted tusks
breaking no water
falling over each other
like actors
in the sawmill

wastepaper icon
        purple and brooding
                doorknob dorsal fin

the mill of familiarity
the elevated contour
blandishment of icicle cigars
the smoldering tip
conceals an elegant
brunette
broom
the chuckling teats
spell disaster

Song for Home

I

the free man
clinging to
an illusory vine
the slave
barking at the gate
neither
knows
what time
it is

II

take it in stride
my friend
it comes around
again

III

to make matters worse
you do your best
tangle the hose
you're a beast
braying at the wind
trickling down
like the sunshine
a glint from
the moon
moving in between
calling out
listening
for a response
slow-moving stream
of light
of forgiving light
that remembers
everything

IV

boy it pays
in dividends
looking to the right
and then the left
leaving homeward
don't it seem
a smiling face
you gather your things
and walk on down
the road again

Much Too Much

I'd readily give
my self if there
was anyone else
or a self to give
yet how can we receive anything
if not through the self?
the rustling of windpipes
refers casually to love
it's supposed to be everywhere
ricocheting between the selves
erected like flimsy statues
reflections of illusion
the birds do not say love
the decision is not there
their beaks clack
soundly
like a darling self
ensconced in gold frailties
and submarine activity
like dynamite
showing a splendor that could not be recognized
except in the spittle that falls when
love is spoken of
abruptly shut
case of fact
nowhere of astral totems

diamond animals
shelter the aimless selves
stupor brings them to the shelf
selfless shelving unit
time's doppelgänger
threatening humanity
with the ripped flag
where love is written
with love it was written
the tartness of these tongues
renders a spell not inside this realm
a picture
perhaps
pleasure of picturing
our future together
when there will be a dead
immobile happiness
sown in plaits like a rose's udders
splayed toward the hoist
moisture is for the eclipsing
the healing of no eclipse
nothing but the kisses
of empty air
where there are no lips
and no intention
spare me and love
but leave it a little illness
for it to fuss obstinately overflowing
flowers water gown
flow blessed relic of the self

and another
neither there
neither here
forest of now
caressing the closed eyelid
of an amalgamation
of dwarf charters
my chute is billowing like a strained
plethora
filtering in the grass dreaded green renegade
nothing opens
it's closed
little selves like flames
litter no interior
because for there to be an inside
there must be something outside
everything operates vice versa
the upholding of a consistent
high-pitched squeaking
like those human peaks
and trouser trout
only able to smell themselves
and the tapeworms dress like hairs
are they plucked
for real
with the tool of the will
that doesn't behave plainly
it displaces
that is the only movement
in this soundlessness

and absolute vision
weather dances stern abreast
the festivities
no one came to witness
no eyes called out to the darkness
seeing is dreamlike in preference
and appeals to the device of its manufacturing
shouting ghost out in outer spaces
the heavy heaven like drapery
spared no expense
accountable
everything is a keyhole
and the self is a key
but it doesn't fit
and both tremble away
serenade the rubble
of eternal affinity
love is a fowl's room
anteroom
shaking thirsty dreams
sooty floor
star-pecked ceiling
the tiles are selves
that fall and smash on the firmament
I know of a few other names
but none of them are the correct one
the only thing is not there
a bull kidney stumps love outright
in fragrant
trepidations

my selves to give
unable to feel the reception
is all over the egg with no being
the eggless fetus
trailing seaweed
the windswept cornices of a polite
palace
decrepit
farm mouse
holy will go wholly
to the hole
underneath the house
where the self and love chase each other's
reflections
in no mirror
no more matter in the mindless gaping
mind fullness of escape
to bright nowhere
please take me forever
I have thanks and snares in my mottled pocked
tickets
up the flume tune it to not the
day of my selfishness
and loose leafed love
tangled hump
the down furled camel
bleats its trumpet and drum
the start of a new thing
the stratum teases tiny tin fingers
fan outward to expel the mole molecules of

lonely inserts
my otherness
friendships setting sun sail
snails in the blue night
drain my dreams until a fork
and gamble is presented to a simple
deafness
absolving deafness
involving blinding height of the
deluded soul strands
like revolving threads in a scientific
desperation
bred in a womb
the empty motherless womb we all share
like a tomb of the earth
our sole breadwinner
our untied shoelaces summertime in a stateless
falling of volume
burlesque of something being there
to begin with
as if nothing could have an end
it's only us
samples of the self
try this try that one
there is a sauce
simmered in celestial spear points
causing the made-up
light to break through the eggshell
darkness
on a distant outer surface

the quiet wrinkles redress the age
the agelessness of marble factories
blurring the sunset out of boundary
the picture frame of the self
no camera exists
to capture whatever is occurring
in itself
love gargles with ink and memory
squids are to be understood as they nest in
love's crevices
nursing the unsung odors that are bred there
untilled ripeness of self
not the right season
I know of no self
and I open my arms the interior appendages
longing to touch something
even itself
not there
heavenly desire running out of steam
the wisps of lost youth
strewn carefully gamut oft mountain frame
oven in nothing baking
beards for the toys unfold
toying with the self
as if there were nothing better
to do
anything does
I'm not lying
I believe unseemly
in the Great Creditor

whose car runs on flukes
on jokester alight and particolored plastic bulbs
of light as fake as fate
as faithful as a sneeze
a blundered grunt of praise
from the scorn and ruby lice
rubbing throats down to the sport
of sperm bathed fretting
allay mating freely
with which to mate indeed
is the bubble on the pot
boils tubing blurt into sand strained
threatened
by self
blithe love lingers like
the most pleasurable one
you can form a dolphin in
two pieces a piece
you see?
I am belief
in you who are
not the only experience I've felt
after a long raining
bowlegged like a sow
ruffle farm herd
ripples delight the ticklish ether
speaking with a tremendous maw
grapes full of corn
or perchance a lace demon
to trickle up the bed post office

yard yank
mine pole in shards of
that which is your favorite
advertising is only a thing
a pasture for trekking nightly
baron
letting go of the formless elves
operating such machinations of love
to you and you alone
only self for you
not me
I didn't write these marks
they're the scratching of a pig
made of rosewater and hemoglobin
goblins
of pleasure
rob us in our
blinding selves
shaking like a shadow
makes not a peep
not a truth is breakfasted bemoaned
because I can't say it
my limp tongue
my sorry condition
I have a load of dirty ball bearings
they are rift in the self
they are a curtain of loving jungle
my owner's judging
jungle aiding abated self
losses too luminous to taste with

a freshly rumored torch
lit someplace else
not such a timely happening
happens
timing is perfected
habitually
gray uniform tenderness
loathing carcasses collated
too lately a
bend green new
it

Proletariat Concern

I am
a big man
between arm of
lover
dappled numerically by caresses
a brightly multiplied
fog
frog of lips
you would be
a sufficient
oil granary
boudoir rounded lovelinesses
askance the
slightest
chance of bears
perforating to be
bringing
lapping majesties
crossed the bed frame
network
tossed out the home
into a barrel window
miniaturized chrome embankment
surrounding file by file
exorbitant draught
the six moon led through florid

deposits
on a silk bar
barcode of my specter
tracing minks traceless milk
wither the
attitude spine
spindles attraction
to grates of poplars' rattle feet
for anterior porpoise to
begin renewal
agitations reckoning fulfill
entry unmoored
sloping basking habitations from one
fortune's
unmasking stand mark
lateral fornication
ornamental
jeweled perimeter
blank fearsome treading
the barometer's
homeward erection
stale stuff
upkeep

License

my urethra
is made of bamboo
for the squirrels
to exchange their
medals
                    a priest up and down
                    in the bathtub
                    full of clay
                    whose resting feet
                    reach up to the
                    little triangles
                    poised bird daffodil
                    poison

A Painting

Above, the murmuring
      sun
      in the sky
      naked of clouds

      whilst in the air
      a bird lilts
      its shadow cast
      directly beneath
      on the wavering surface
      of the ocean

      below,
      a fish hangs in the water
      as if glued
      to the spot

      a traceless line
      passes through all of them
      it's lovely

I Take This Bear As My Bride

my lapsing broom
pushed together
like a faucet
out of which comes
my bear without any bread
a tattoo haloed around its crest
it fogs the windshield masterless gazed
a croak lies on the stretcher
taken away
washing
tyrants infant plaster bastardizing lope
who don't move their arms and
legs
been keeping it for awhile yonder
and pulleys ropes hydrangeas squid
squeaking hair
applied later
to my honey-blotched
thighs
cellular winking apron
at disposal
climb up to the celestial tumor
an airplane and a star are making dough
the satellite watches
hungrily unaware
are you or aren't you

my leaf clobber
my lunar hells
my flanges
drip the humor luck
mince mince
fell over
let it freely

The Cat

slinking pleasurably
downward
decry the fervor of the
rippling fruit
that droop
frequently onward
for the goad
flour involves
flour presses the necessity
of a gilded
lining
framework home
a miner sounds his horn
redeemable at the corner
untie the dawning
of pleasant juries
leaden juices perking
a pale
remorse
fraudulent doll scape
rigging the demoralization
of plenty more to store
eat the banner upon which outer
words are smitten
remedial flickering

untitled 3

In a field which resembled a courtyard
the motes of dust went along lazily
in the warm spring air
some were laughing
others crying
and singing
one assumed the shape
of a rhinoceros' horn
and yet another
the form of a lamp
two decided to join together and made
a beautiful feast
but the particles of its aroma
distressed the motes
lightning flared
like nostrils
eggs broke open
caresses went a roving
and all the motes became
fists aimed at the heavens
"never again shall we return to dust!"
they cried
and they
didn't

Suspension

the cache is indelible
it delegates the
concierges
the soap mobile
rides upright
and even as I write this
nothing is changed

gently sliding haze
of snow
rotund snowman
melting silently in the
sunlight

heavenly brown
tourist body
sticking in a
glistening trap

heavenly postman
let me kiss your onions
you deliver my mail
every day

the hugeness evaporated
a lavender quail takes place

along the pedestrians

if only to see
the tea of light
filling the cup
of your eyes
empty and full
where a porcupine
guards the jewels
covered in honey

the monkey
ribbon
wears cataract suspenders
a dark stream
unfolds
amidst the falling
blossoms

heaven
shining through the keyhole
like a woman
of ghosts

Everything Gives Me A Bath

police are
seeking
a woman
in connection with the
murders of twenty
thousand tentacles
where the minuscule
tap water of your
dreams
comes trickling out
like a runny nose
a nose running
in the dark
to escape
the concentric elopers
who mimic so precisely
an infant cactus
placed in a drawer
around my head
wide open
my mouth smiling umbrella
my eyes winter coat
my hands in a field
surrounded by growths
important people
administrative
release

Two Beliefs

slimy slug
makes a wet mark
slimy slug
in the stars
all too briefly
collapse into the Host's lungs
which convert cellulose
into
cameras
a camel takes a picture
of the Eiffel Tower
it's a garden plant
invested in the rainfall
that collects
in the casement
the mind's brassiere is too tight
the bas-reliefs are fascinated
and dissolve upon reaching
      the ground

Oil

snake water
rinses my succulents
perched on a dove
extracting its tusks
deftly
with my ears
crowning achievement
lying down on my back

I cry out of my knees
into the lackluster

the pilotless
drone
gives an excellent blowjob

multiply my eyes by a thousand
and that's where you'll find my mouth

I cry out
of my knees
into the lackluster appraisal

Aristotelian Subcontractors

aloft the
degenerate gorilla flesh
dark brooding
muscle
pressed face
against grain
teeth

Christmas
in potato
cremation in
potato
bright lamp-like cabbages
docile
becalmed
the lights like flies
hump around
beneath snow
ape flesh
the figures are kept
in the shed
to later be put in the fields
my life is a stem
God the rhinoceros
playing video games
at the alter
every drop of water is separate
like time
the plum I have just eaten
the plum I shouldn't have

Full

knocks the vase onto the floor
pushes the statue into the pudding
tips the dangler over the edge
floats beside the bridge
tying a long string of yarn
around a package
turning the little windmill
touching the tip of a hummingbird's beak
rubbing a millipede up and down
soothing a tarnished blight
startle the affairs
start the triumphs from afar
lubricate the enemy
purse inside-out
barnacles suck against the underbelly
of a sore
strained girth
palpitate in the nursery
prolong
scuba driver
in the round
all round all white
allocation of blasted
hunger pangs
groan stomach
loan features
elastic curving
extricated from a thorn

Abject Sphincters In Dire Hatred

brutally meticulous
the hand
protruding out of an oyster
there are rings
on its fingers
when it shuffles them around
there is a loud ringing

the first is an acorn
pupil in the
dolphin
though dolphins don't have puppets
the second membrane
emits a large
thirst
the balcony is coughing
there are hyenas
on the razor blades

the human being
endlessly peeling its skin
it lays them down
on little inside-out baby swigs

good night
aloe sun
a dark cloud
in the nowhere
of space
trickling fingers
ant desires
nowhere sun
on board

Thus Function

home is where your
heart-God is
that God of hearts
consoling
inconsolable one
with
diminishing returns
feeds all that it touches
with the warmth
of a breast
that cascading
ever-loving milk
of light
over all
the folds
that bathe us so sweetly
flower petal God
counseling my soul
into ever leaving
or into ever returning

Plurality

walk across
the room
to each other
the sewing needles
peck the floor
deliberately
statues to lay flowers
and the phony
pliancy
of the air
the air of this town
this town full
of air
to bed
quickly

the brain goes
smoothly in its tube
lightning in the distance
paths of insects
something is underway
mouthing
delicate scabs

having to force
the little strata
of excrement
from my
bowel
by pure strength
of will

Thorough

I prefer
to live closer
to the skin of life
with its austere
and simple pleasures

when alone
refine yourself
to be in the company
of others

ceaselessly refining
away
until there is nothing left
but yourself

honed to an infinitesimally sharp point
enough to rob a fly of its wing
in midair

I do not want to eat
until I am glazed over
nay,
I want to get life
by itself
to be alone

itself
with no adornments
or filters
the self by itself
outgrown
alone

I'll let the others
look at my life
I don't need it
all is free

if you want to spend your time
remembering
that's your business
not mine

Hands of Plenty

when one happens to spy
two similar bugs
making their way
along the ground
how can one be certain
that they have anything to do
with each other?
are they siblings
or acquaintances
or is life to them
a giant byway
along which they perhaps
jostle each other and bump
but each keeps to
their own world?
and a third bug appears:
how wonderful!
how dismal!

My Diary!

the idiot smiling child-face
of a dog
the quiet and persistent
disobedience
of child-cats
she-apes
with measured gait
tightest embrace
the pine trees
little men alight
from the branches
on the periphery
like doves
their blue
downward cast
shadows
tear multicolored leaves
on the
streets
patrol

when something's up
you've got to tell me
I can't guess at it
I would go on thinking

that nothing's
wrong

making bare intimations
on the floor

there are higher
learnings
at stake

go on making height
for the spaces
pheasant weather
the jeweled void
transparent discrepancies
at a touch

don't interrupt the
man
learning to drown
at the seashore
alone in the foam
floundering from one
flower to
another
the next room
in the compartment

untitled 4

your brain batch of cookies
humane society
and a splendor of
civil wars
given bouquets
circling above the
meeting
place
a pair of pants
surveillance state
of mind

untitled 5

pin clothing
to heaven
the roundness
evaluates
feeling it
oat of shape
for many wranglings
finger
discussing disgusting
plant ham
orders of the
bake
cake of decay
furnace

the stolid
bullfighter
thusly disrobes
tremors
make charcoal
harbor
covering
his skin
skinny

My White Bailophone

in the breeze

enough to run
slight along
the course

talking matter
stops
every drop is
eventual
a cormorant spreading
in the snow
of dark
reflexes
anonymity
frequent flags lashing out
lines of creases
steam

untitled 6

two complete men
standing near to one another

surrounded by a layering of
indistinguishable landscape
out of doors
trees perfume the air
at a distance
a road
those ubiquitous
yet insipid
alterations to being's
display

sometime later
they begin to converse
the drafty diamonds huddling
at the tip of raised branches
listening
to the twittering humans
who make wet splats
with their forward
holes
falling from their
summit

in summation
for it were summer
anew

It

I

the
ciudad de
San Juan
roosted firmly
atop
sobre de la mesa
aqui
translates to the
goat
'here'
in swishing blade
across gentile enough
forlorn the
loose spiders
ribbing a web
until its
toast
anchovies lobe
red quite under a
drawn blue summer
the some merciful
outer otter tittering
fodder

of mammal madder male
float ablaze the
great city
distraction is a
jowl
eunuch ugly
celestial formality
formaldehyde incest
step right hearing
aids and dressings
San Juan
peopled by
luscious space
spoken in words
that manage the
dust which blinks
waiting past the ages
for the only gesture
to be
a forever
awful return
peephole
precise
brought itch
parcel
for an everything
liaison
form of poor
detest
destitute

longer
longitudinal
plead holes give sigh
lozenge
of peony pleasant
it friends
to a butter
mistletoe
hen laid
preternatural
broach its
cone
a silo distinct
family maid cone
down the
chime of bell door
wingtip
droll popping mouth
behold
bees gather each mold
fabrication
a laid crater
too a waste

II

the whole
has not a speck
of hesitation
never sneezes
coughs unto itself

it is just itself
there isn't a
place
for fear
or worry to tarry

the world carries the world
it is a world
and another
which lays on top
of the other

they look the same
down to the drifting
hair
borne on the wind
waded through by
an isolated
wing

words describe
these
as
two
worlds
but they are delicate
laced together
without a seam

remember this
there is not something
able to tear
not a moment
of waxing
or waning

that there is
waiting
is silly

a child
gurgling
water

everything bears the seal
like an identity
a reeking faucet
a stolen ounce of waste
prevails
regularly

slitted into the far
descending crevices
of two eyes
not placed
boundless open mouth
nothing to consume
swift removal
of in and out
oats soiled
sown
sold
home
dwindling thither

store cove
often revealing
marble beautiful slabs

lathering this now
over every place
is the same
devoid of distance
devout trembling tear
cross
cross again
like rockets

suchness of
industrious
ants

the struggle
crowned
humanity
glistens
of no moisture

just a dry
soundless
dreaming
between the two
worlds
is pronounced
space

doves float
after
about
love you
all inability
straying in a stable
none at all
wears constancy
flattened jewels
propo
banana peels

give it a sign
flash of symbol
it would

be difficult
to discern
otherwise
signpost

the absent
thing makes
distraction
without object
abject substance
stale perceiving
breaks like a wave
a product babe
itches each aisle

the two worlds
seem like only one
but neither
one or two
goes along glowing
wishing crying hopeful
to see
the other thing
just outside

a notice of rain
less scaling flying
falling
but whither?
whence?

when?
ever and ever
a haven bedecked
with clovers
overt
erect
onward detection
suspect
overload
lord in the garden
fragrance of
the wondrous
something
which any word
merely slaps against
and drowns
downward
spiders
fullness of spiraling
anywhere spending time
thrift
adrift the lame thoughts
puttered
out like smoke from
a locomotive
produced by the
ineffable snoring
cretin

putrid
satisfaction
flits from grasp
as a rheumy shadow
that is spared
by colon
by breading teeth
mewling yawn gaped
suckle berry
at the harm
of cause
no more principles regain
standing formula
elation
patent severed patience
limes up indoor rows
the defiant meanings
clawed apart the jungle
this reality
it grows right back
nether monuments delay
a backdraft
slim pickings
to ooze from
moon warbling tides
a bit of cat
exposing every time

the steel
ironing board

metal
railing
is arbitrary
like pretending
like believing
love is a truant
police farm
bubbling sternly
out of manifold breedings

there is no
giving and

there is no sound
collared living
noting death has little
to clasp

the figment
idol
useful as a doorknob

above the taut sails
a flock of
dreams form a
barbershop
in the furrowed
cleft

holding on is
a ghost
and letting
go is
a dull
miscommunication
breast

putting on clothes
what humiliation
what drainage system
flourish
like bowers

Known More

thought leads to but two outfits
fatal to wear in adequate positions
thinking draws a path
on one pointed end
a deep interior personal
Divine
Truth
locked in place
by everything
whose form is how it's pronounced
the language is any boulder raining
on the other's root
is infinity
whose namelessness is
Chaos and the mystery
that is endless confusion
isn't one of the direct links
impressionable
or nautical radium for
the blue fuel
insert them each
the roiling tube
of not any
car growls

Sterling

slowly dawning
the awareness of
retractable pincers
lowing out of the dark
to hang perhaps
linens upon
iron hair braids
daintily defecate inside
defeated miseries
collecting on a single point
pinched like a rub
the spoiled hub
of lightning granary
canaries

gander my setting steeds!
they align like sweetest porcelain
aged crooked refrain
hold forth your trepid elation
muffled catastrophe
apocryphal
just absurd
no footfall to pedal
an escaped host
yowling
softly the machinery like rain
firm rainbows lash firmament totals
calculated
fur trees infinity

Knick-Knacks

when amidst the marching feet
that are the moments
of the day
hiding in the open
should you
for a chance
and a reason
raison d'état
ministers crouch the bird long marshes
bust
billow opening
nearing open window
trace your spouse
species remind you
inordinate thresher stole
the wheat
the calf of wheat
tearing upper cruise
repair to the cysts
over-hooking the avalanche
it's backwards
hiss time replenishes all the steam
leeching away winter
yards are all over the game
plan it oar your oat
sleep eatery give a break a beep

urgent team
fortune the gore
wide horizon
opening it seamlessly
in winter
outer through door remote
is their tether
bankers a must
price may be variegated
armoire
battered by the infantry
militant the butter
from afar
is rubbed
red again
or actual
no colored
checkered turns about
finding its footing
a home
lone pulp
spared eagerly
from the snow boned over
the snails which reenact a windmill
of their own
erection
recollect the taxation's pains
somebody musk feel for them all
the feeders rubber snow
rain deer snot bundles

gathered well
knell
rest
delightful feather
jutting out of no hair
where else wood be droning on on on mono
on yum autonomous my kiss a friend
fried a fiend
fecund kettle
of your desire
my finest
triangulate
the police
twisting their glowworms
'round the streetlamps
seething light
like an apostrophe
the miser egg cradle is distortion
a blooming thunder
head bloody helping
mate your apes are quelled
intestine drapery of the torso
or so belongs
meow enow
mind your own danger
I can inflict my own
toils
foils oft coiled in flit utter care
lay the snare for me
to dawdle my knee

mittens given to nieces
atop geese
measly
dappled caboose
swelling
disdainful air
my hare
you there
theirs is youth
its palapa
unravel your umbilical
suture
the moisture is steady
a drafty steed clipping the fragrant grass lashes
to be a prettier being
dew wiped slavish attire
the applicator is in the back grounding
a pearl onto the landing
which could be or is if
deer
tremble
drawn oarsman
pope idiot glen placement
mattress of mutual fabrication
applications attend to all yard borough
numbing burgers
food pears dredge
my sludge dragon
hammer droplet
upon the rings of satellite ticking

hoops to play
with remodeled voidness
flat
untied
untoward
greening
flume
nip the eternity switch
ephemeral artery

Cloud

everlasting
traveling in an elevator
a plain bug
interior
curtain polite
telephone meter
at myself
the fragrant delivery
of a separate place
more word juice
mourn
the lewd morning ankle
flecked an open-air
slit
that place was shown me
the air is a miraculous height and
tenderness
fish like fruit
glaze the lead bellies
of the clouds
overlooked cloudy day frame
step insert
plead
step insert the border folly
of often bright
mind toad

hiccupping its muses
with smoke
nostrils related tendrils
abscond my loved objection
subject me this phantom hole
space
wanted more to go here
and any hair else
the matter
after toot and pail
I assail my glass beaded
lozenge
longer thoughtless lounge
grace fully proud
and full
fuel of might
mightier of steam swarm
dotting arid face pressure
pink junk surprises
of my life
in a gown
warble neck straps
picking loose
pickle
loser young fooling around about face
texture it right and sand
sanded beam brings me found a sample
at the place whichever
exchanges
the noon tide drown

the drawn moose pile drowning
spitter coffee chamberpot
and whose
onto first lathe
benign agape
again
the featuring stork
regaled rafter gallstones
sister of thirst
night thinks abroad

                    drink

The Fortress At Night, After

the form of what constitutes sight
avails my looking around
for the equivalent of myself
interior picture frame
that my scattered attention keeps erasing
forever
or it is uncovered in the sand
halfway eaten by angelic crabs
the pristine awareness
of their retractile mandibles
fills the valise with cognac
fills out the ledgers with foolproof chicken
scratches
at the dawn
the renewing day
we are forced to endure
like a mirage
dancing from tip to tip
of eyelashes
boats press the foam toward an
open hound
a wound guessing the stratagems
gems of fragments
owls wink at me behind my ears
I let them in my looking around
the aimless pursuit

change dropping its clothes in heaven
bowls
bluebird split open spilt yolk figs and clinging
beetles
dampened with mascara
and toothlessly afloat
float some
flotsam bride
you are never found
it is too hard to be earnest
better is it to be a half self
carrying through each obligation
while the deeper half rests invisible
in truth
sliding remotely out of reeking fingers
dingy pleasure
the rowing of fingers groping the formless
truth
one or two
more than myself
is enough
my self
isn't merry
to begin with
I've forgotten
what to do
with this clumsiness
brick tar hand ruling outer mouth
loser lunatic baedeker freak breakage tonight
onion love

peeling feelings lemurs
peelings
leaving them all
behind
in the compost heap
of the self
what can grow here
what will can be
to make such a decision
liver debts
unruffled payments cement
mixer of my longing
mine look
across the gales
betook the nook rook hook right up tuning
hurl
ice is gone to bark
puke grossly
out from in
furthermore, from out
never where mind less and anchovies
beside
toilet pool
swims and twirls
friend
shipping helmets
haven't you met
and boots
in the heat
fitted to each anteroom ghost

the mob progress
parallel to oblivion
striping acorn furnishing ethernity
after twelve
thirty
yearlings deceased
disused easel aisle cease
protraction figure complete with model bones
complimenting hairline iris sigher bedecks
crucifixating a lope
gnome
trickle my rocks and my grass strand to upset
the hen
and make an emitted rune moan
spurned spurts blossom educated advances
rain maintain breading braid

Shouldn't Have

the curvaceous truth
standing waist length
grasses swinging light fixation
travail
vast veil
under the hooting hail markers
a bread stone ghost
of truth
reconstructing its reflector
a gain
to soothe
more so
left overwhelm foot pedals fasting hard beat
harnesses bleating blue eardrum
blood descended
louts antler room scale
middling weight
write it downward
into you
losing pole
filmy bulb
gaunt
red bridge
yearn
rank smell
learning

more heaven
to spare tirelessly
somber tired
tried binocular
thrice whistle mice blend
lend characters
forlorn argument
felled by the stream
that minces in a moon hat
eye beam
closet yourself
further
fur shields you yet
letting yeti
no makeup believe ewe mean
plants untold pantaloons
two uses form a bird
a blown lone
blower holy umpire empress
heaviness impresses meat eyes sorely
souring hay frail and darkener
monday together forage the heather
sweeps the corridor less nominally than uses
please untie the duvet
uttered dove reeds four find sing stress me
pleats
plaits lank lender
mothering leadened
mourning ardor
or is it

arbor
articles cloth mood silk
freezes press around the neck
knifed goat home
horn loan
fuel inside each other school
hoop loosely blackened blurred biddy features
undo mid tight
right papers rights rice lapels bright house
lousy witch spigots
ruining fueled reverie hair
mateless breeds coup to cooperate adjunctly a
quarter
peach

untitled 7

like the leaves of an aspen
everything shimmers
an endless golden
glimmering
the depthless illusion
empty as a skull
as meaningful as death
going on
alone or together
we fall to the floor
in a pool
of sunshine
and milk
that becomes as butter
upon its penetration

Ego or
Such Indulgence

around midday this
day of a
year
at the convergent sidewalks
swaddling two streets
in this city
where a pair of glasses
float away
also
inert a bottle swayed
inside out
giving rise to profile
of whitening soundless wigs
sallying gourd
under roots
begging to be seen
the feeling grown out of a tree
in the law
yonder the park
where twining lovers molt gaily
their stamps indomitable gray
total unbelievably whittled
the rinds renovate each proposed nursing
sight is hurtful
deer sprint fragility down the lanes

the corner of the city
walked transparent and airy
toppling anchors
from high outlets
rib of cloud flattens the early earth
quilted ruby the leverage days
dye a cordial flour bell
sneeze cause of perpetrating the spoon fellows
alone
loud lonely reels
grunt growl was the bakery issued
upon earnest
partitions
stout advocate nation pride lifting up
healing the slime
behind it
exiles
freely
to be domed
a heard heaven
hindquarters aflame of ears
neck lied
to head start
blame a desirous
control
blind what can be identified
grab in all directions plaintively
remind the rubbing clean
of conscience
the sign planted at the

limit
gives off the
words
STOP AT THE BEGINNING
the rest is false
impossible to match
its pace
just be borne along
thitherward
where you are
and happy presents
sliding door moments
stubbing the self
on its
toes
if only there was an ending
but it trails off
speeding
oozing
never fading
only our attention wanes
nothing else
we wallow luxuriously
we allow our hands to let it go
our minds to release
the little prey
only to be caught again
that rascal self
merging into shadow
making again its entrance

a new character but the same tired actor
underpaid

every mind
is the same
mind
just as
all fires
are but one fire
coming out of
different orifices
then returning to its
real home
the one darkness
bubbling with one light
flickering wavering
senselessly struggling
without goal
that is the nature of desire
of the world
wrapped around the mind
never touching
so far distantly removed
that not even a faint dwindling echo
can breach the shore
cold home
warm heaven
own hell lonesome ownership
pilot possessing
lovely tumbling around

no fear of bumping up against
anything
else
foolish limping fire
the perfect demonstration
of the will of existence
the height of animation
reality handicapped and deformed
boundlessly actual
disgusting reminder
of our folly
our rude and inconsiderate bumbling
of limbless trunks pulsing
and accusing
making terrible ugly faces oil the very end
the true mind
drunken foul dispersing obscenities
with the only sincerity that's possible
fear confusion impatience
reveals the human in every mind
the gawking looping human
complete with man-made mind
no refund guarantee
we are already caught
oorving out the sentence
in imaginary isolation
and tears bulging forth despite
restraint
it is only the unintentional
the impulses

reaction the only inmost breath of the
missing
self
coughing silently out
the shadow
that is our experience
waning and waxwing in the sun
the looming leering sun
changeless originator of time
ripping a new tear
at every
inanimate moment
a totem tottering
the human face is scarred
by preference
excuses excuses excuses
the deepest belief
a garbled message
response to receiving the award
the big reward
most charming
most athletic
most interesting
most important
most authoritative
peerless
study pattern for the
future
obligations
nothing lives in memory

we won't know or feel
after the time receding spares the
cosmological feelers
tremble like a babe
raising by the wind
a catalyst for heaving time across the gap
made-up
forged
lodged in dreams passing
like a rainbow
into the bowel of living health
dig it
upwards and downstairs
the antelope saunters figuratively demon
clover
laden with rides
across a soothing lassitude depleted vows
checkpoints marking the passage of
baseless thoughts
careen thoroughly full
and through
it's up to you
to efface the rabbits
silhouette of truth
figureless dawning
of it
you
me
overt diversion
heading for a headless fountain glowing brain

tag your itch spit
the crater at the middle portion
evenly distributed
every parcel of space
eats of the intangible meal
we strive to taste
and imagine that we do
but for us it can only resemble
memory
feelings
experience
the blind hammer
crawling like a slug
dullard druggist dunk herd
arrow bend
swelter
faster

I am just an outlet
trying not to interfere
with the activity of the
indistinguishable location
where everything joins with me
if I try to feel it
my awareness covers it
like a damp cloth
stained with
blood
petal-shaped tear drops alone and amassed
semen broken off from solitude

anxiety like a delicate murder
cannot be stopped
I can only slide with it
parallel
I can't keep up
too much to remember
memory is not the self
the self is stuck in the present
the presence of time
similar to a noise from the next room
a creeping burglar
prowling around
with no intention of stealing
steps aside to avoid the searching
beam of light
sight
ear and ear poised acclimating to hearing
what is to be heard
without a picky self
a sticky grossly clothed self
dirt and grit
betwixt teeth
hovering in the dark
you can't be certain they're still there
you can only rely on memory
and it's false
falsehood itself
interpretation a waste of life
endless invisible moment
like a ceaseless dry cleaner's conveyor belt

each garment strikes and passes through you
there is no finer material
than that of time
as soft as heaven
as discreet as a child born from a maid
lifelong maid caring for the exterior
leaving the interior to trickling against the
grave weight of being
all weight
and expansion
collecting in a single point
you
me
the other people are capable of becoming
ideal
super marvel grand ribald fire bolt fabrication
the action of time
a continuous weaving
of the static
security
without despairing
continuous unraveling
simultaneously
everything every thing and
nothing no thing
snow blowing in the liberating space
a trailing veil
our bride is retreating
into the furnace of memory
the human heart

I'm trying to tell you
about myself
I think you are like me
how could you be different?
aren't we all natural
organic
effulgent
indulgent arrogantly gallivanting
like we knew what was happening
and how we belong
I can't understand in my body that there
is no dilemma
no problem was ever real
mystery solved
dissolved in memory
and the self
the twinkle of particles
like sand in the beautiful cosmic
void
that's the ultimate thought I can muster
stuttering and shaking the urine
off the slit at the end of my
imagination
I can dream up a self
but it's gone the next day
and I can barely remember
anything
I want you to confirm that what I experience
is accurate
and how I feel is correct and just

justify my dangling saliva
ham
the gold password lapsing through
the jewel of now
feathers shaking the ridge of time
rugged terrain
everything takes the same effort
nothing is different
sameness is naked and dangerously revealed
to the blinking mirror
the reflections stick and pile up and become
obscure
gray
smushed together
stranded on the vast mote of dust
smaller than can be conceived
is this interesting
worth the invaluable experience of it
though it won't remain
maybe some of me
what I hope to be truth
will ride out the tide with you
in a recess of your mind
as part of your living
share our living parts
the sensation of touching something
that is touching you
because it wants to
to feel
a truth

dressed like you
but distinct
always weather hereafter

how wonderful
to be sincerely listened to
and validated by the purposeful
intention
of the same mind
beyond control
celebrated for living the right way
good job bravo
that's how to do it
enjoyable to watch be a part of
our mind peeks into the holes of our eyes
trying to witness
the self
outside
certainty security comfort
the morsels a self drools and trips over
but they are a mirage
in the desert of the self
throat parched
lungs burning
alive but vainly
an attempt nothing more

when you die
you won't feel if someone
remembers you

you're not there
life is not in the mind of somebody else
and it's not in your mind either
it's just your experience right this second
fraction of a second
the gait of time
millisecond
quarter of a millisecond
fragment of an atom of time
whirling motionless and placeless
there are no seeds
no growth
no vessel for decay to find activity
remoteness of tired eyeballs falling
gracelessly
bottomless pit
mouthless pit of eternity
abyss of infinity
deposits the stench of its waste
just to tease us
into opening again
the self
the never-before-seen object
bloated mass of reality
hands swipe through it
as if it were
smoke
trading forms with the sky
if only for
a moment lifetime

ago
longing to appear
in full honest nudity
the real self
full whole handsome strength
regale gala parting boudoir
what we can remember being promised to us
is lost in memory
here it is
from the empty beginning emanation
disguised as the real
thing
limitless joy of being the only one
that everybody loves to have sex with
the best lay
indefatigable lover
everyone's secret mistress
evolved to remain high above every other
person
praise to this self
the only one
the one who knows you
in your inner faintly glow
alone the foremost road
to haphazard leverage
lip the switch swatch it foully pellet fowl
raising the trees in affluence
because of the effect that you cause
that you are the only cause of
the spring of truth

a sprig
just get to know me
then you will agree
I am yourself
I volunteer to take the helm
on everybody's behalf
never to be besotted by corruption
temptation is a mirror that has captured a
reflection
that appeals to your reality
frogs have legs
to be dinner tablets fold over the moon grave
stone
ethereal tombs
the pollution of time
a vacant storage facilitation
move to the next lot
no morning or time down is allotted you
mewling elk
so cute
that instinct to love the little selves garbed in
fur
it can't help but just be cute
it's surviving to receive love
the only thing that can penetrate the blindness
of the self
before it turns its ray again today
wayward beam of intention
let the line out
all the way

what a catch
eat drink feeling yourself honestly
without the carbonated dragon pattern border
terrapin
something that does not need use
the necessary changes
the useless and superfluous
flourishes wildly like a jungle
unread instruction manual of being
our understanding merely skims the pages
that are torn out
and answers each prayer with an excuse
a reason
a human being who doesn't brush the
tremulous relationship
that is reality

life isn't here just so I can feel
profound
and perfect
correct innately important
in regards to what
one day a year
a person will be elected to serve as
golf
they are what the world depends upon
for the day
selfishness as the way to happiness
only it must be voluntarily relinquished
tread the water of your patience

until your muscles burst against the stars
and make them thump with
envy
you've got
yes, you
that one more distinguished than the others
your servants
you are the receiver of effort
the rest of them inflate your balloon
every hand claps every mouth cheering polite
belief
in you
the sole
substance
the remainder
glory be to you
you who are the only self
every me
the anticipator of every decision made
cake of delight
upright music of solvents preternatural
dismantled belch

supreme entity that is reality
tell me that you love me
and that every single twitch and movement
is as it should be done
take me to the kitchen so we can be alone
and reveal your approval of me
my every instance and development

nothing could be a mistake
if it was performed by me

wherefore the mind
if its only function is to lie
steal swindle
what does proof resemble
who obtains the truth
the truth will change
everything thinks the self
but the branches scratch the windowpane
of the self
tickling the underbelly
of the soul
accidentally exposed
to its mother substance
father material
the winding world twittering at your head
source of all precise judgement
and supreme authority
I'll make this a great story
leave me in charge
unseen
like a god
fooling around in the voided place
no return
but what to return to?
nobody lives where you want to go back to
they're carried along with you
everyone shares the same opportunity

for running upon the startled steps of a true
pyramid
axis of power
stripped naked
bowling alley
frequently damp
with cat pistols and stamens made of rain
sandstone births
occurring opulently and faithful to the fashion
society bespoke the warm word eager for a
hearing
a lasting self
outlaw gunning foe bone
this may seem like self-centered nonsense
irrelevant to the actual physical toiling of
lives
but it shares its meaning
I have meaning
so do you
from the same batch
equal meanings
popping like firecrackers
everywhere
a mind is brewing
trying caring meaning to do whatever it is
that you are currently doing
it's not for you or someone else
it's the only thing
it is what you feel
what you just felt

fading away slowly
into reality
save this chicken soup
preserve this so I may know
what I once knew
and fondle angrily
the shape of truth
now dispersed
by the fog of time
the scream etched city
where the master of control fits his phallus
into the hole
designated Other
reaping the harvest
that which we sow
the self
imagining the future never stopping
and containing a proud self
still the self
fulfilled satisfied
no more work or strife
you completed it
you discovered the ultimate meaning
that the self wants only for recognition
beyond error
that no one can find fault with
just that the self is right
in whatever it happens to be doing
a moment is not long
a self is not substantial

being is not accessible
things remain active changing identities
a hundred thousand times per microscopic
unit of time
that lizard
cruising the gallbladder of sacredness
as it was thought before
so it is thought now
wherefore is the thought or thinking
that was never discovered?
how to elicit what was
never before?
the self
wants
to be new
brand new and instantly fastidious
dull feeling
it is self fishing for a complementary
adulator of itself
it knows that it once knew things it now
considers childish and amateur
dumbly acquired
now if the new knowledge
whose object is the subject
which is empty
illuminated absence
that's all the world is
put all you clutch into the world
fill it
with your loving self

saturated self
feels only deserving of the most immortal
reputation
the living creature which evolved
intentionally to the archetype in the sky
railing slid down
coat heels flickering behind
supported even by the wind
blossoming around aboard the tides
the self's personal chauffer
coffee? ice? relief?
anxiety removal
cream of weakness?
gibbon of licking swiftly
the fraudulent dorsal fin
sprung from an insect of elephantine
dimensions
coming forward from behind your back out of
your understanding
you can see whatever you like
but it's only the self
shifting sameness cracked
apart like an anemone
desirous of its just desserts
frozen candied truths
in a wrapping of meaningful movement
earmark your rotted hook
read the mindlessness of the self
acting through

another
always reaching the same aim
the goal is identical
despite the bulbous eyes that gape at it
from every direction opinion reason
experience
that tingling
the world
the self thinks it can find something
in the world
which contains everything
if it's not here
you wouldn't know it
kiss my words gently
it is my love passed this way and that
wanting a receptacle
and reciprocation

do not listen to your mind
it will misuse you
it has its own agenda
(your 'I' is showing!)
but it is only you
who can feel the consequence
a witness to your own life
a rollercoaster pulling you
regardless of direction
naked of meaning or purpose
agile in its insignificant
being

Spoken Word Poem
for the Deaf and Blind

sounds are merely another
jeweled distraction
giving another imaginary dimension
to delusion
as for your sightless eyes
don't make up a world that isn't there
that isn't how they tell you it is
there is only one thing to see
but we can only glimpse a figment
of its shadow
as it bounds
heavenward
within that which experiences
beyond it
beyond where things are
look where nothing is
where words disappear and the only sound
is that which emptiness makes
clattering within itself
vessel of every nothing and every something
makes quite a bundle
the string must needs be pulled tight
knotted further
otherwise
something or other will happen

the real willst wilt asunder
and sleep comes only
to those who awake
disgusting burst of flame
sleep
a taste of true rest
teasing miser
won't let us indulge in a gram
of getting out of this mess
hall of history buried in time
nothing but dreams and illusions come out
like a mummy
who has no slippers
bug frost teeth
and scaling the highest temple testicles
abound noisome and quavering
bears mold each darling into a scum
fitting for petulant belfries
mineshaft wherein the fiends dig at the
surface only to discover
further surface

untitled 8

a deeply tumbling cloud
shivering up from the crease of the
perfumed horizon
where the metallic eyes are lined up
where honey oozes
from the glorious opening
the angular tides
pause upon meeting each other
suspend the cash
the roaring and the foam
quick as a bulk
several times in a row
like dummy horses
quivering in cold folds
drapery of malignant depiction
outstretching its foliage
litter hewn cleft on the land
recede, scapes
rescind
grope your funnels
swiftly in the velvety sneezing
caused by a ripped
tank
ploughing through the sleeping dust
whipping with its engorged trunk
a beauty

a ribbon flapping lethargically
upon its gleam
a gleam as of a goat
put up to cost
a fullness breasts cough
flowers a lad before noon

Something To Work Toward

A monk/nun is one
who has let go
of the self
released the burden
of body and mind

who is unattached
not bound
by other people
nor by objects and things
not bound
by the mind's habits and
constructs
nor by ideas and
opinions

who is immovable
unaffected
by the stirrings of the world outside
and the thoughts inside
who is without vanity
and self-image

a monk/nun
is not caught up
in frivolous, superficial

activity
does not engage
in self-centered striving
and pleasure-seeking

who gives no thought toward
fame and renown
much less gain and
loss
and for whom the
past, present and future
are as leaves
tossed about by the
wind

the life of the
monk/nun
is given for the sake
of all beings
is the manifestation
of the One Activity
of True Nature
the flowering of
No-Self
the boundless embrace
of Love

Silence

For You

I saw myself clear as in a mirror
I imagined that my dreams were true
I beheld a pregnant reality whose womb
bore myself
yet within I tossed and turned
I shuddered and cried
I wore a nameless pain howling like the
darkness of night
a creature drew itself forth
and stabbed against a stone
with every centimeter
its tightness of strength
creation
every libation
motor
clobber
but I am just another
like myself
it is only my memory
which holds the scars of my anguish
and my heart
ripped asunder
by imageless hands
my own

Steering Wheel

but first course
to test the readily harboring ambulation
trying the response in exposed flesh
ready-made
can it stir this up delicately
a noxious stupor
or a port of gainly
yarn
whining the ears hear not a rubble
neither rumors flit the rehearsed air
lapping from the creases of the stable
rudiments these hoses crest a bask
rooftop of glamour and glares
habits of the hands
they handle the action to produce
these ill polluted terms and jets of digits ink
spits
a fresh jar
from the minnow gaze thimbles nitty griping
jetties
polite too nice
the rays under strands storming the opera
barge
too undisclosed to think little puppies
droplet

octogenarian seeding the runny brood beyond
yokes astride
a power to tweak the hams
flatten thistles blade keys on tut toy yowl orb
subordinate
it
gotten
place of butter
glands
hymen width clams
blot hands some time aglow

Himself

the bleating of a moment
resembles masterly a thrown away
reflection in unseen mirror
my image
I cannot see it
I look to others
their eyes are closed
licking fearsomely lips ragged with
consumptive opposition
to nothing
but themselves
I look into a mirror
myself
and see the peopled world
winding homeward

the cadaver of the self inside the interior
impregnable eye
wishes it could dumb and shameless
stampeding through the pilgrimage
but I have cradled more than my share of
guiltiness
like an empty seagull in my foam
I can stop caring
habitual tendons rip and share the filth frame
overdeveloping us all over

in the lake of cow
lowly upturning the mood
lessons fish eared tune outing brook bathers
eyelids wave
length
the shadow bounding against
everything that is a mirror
everything else without staleness
and trembling tears front
face me in the mirror
the part of me that is everyone
I try to touch down
but my foot brushes the air
cleanly
resting in pleasing ease
water is wasted in protein gangs
and grain garish
grab garbling hunker
plow mowing
mooing blood peels orangutan sage grapes
twin little tryst
dinette now in mediate future

Sample

precisely
a point
divided on either
side
a lizard's tail
splits
covering a
desire
with the flesh-like
threshold
beacon that blossoms
through the
perforated colander
handed me
the carven shield
to deflect
this gaseous humongous
affront
at the back gate
the cat
licking at its rail
waiting to be let
in
door handle
it none too widening
mount

Tenderly Listing

sending sight through the clever
opening
as for the hands
a cane will be there
to acquaint them with placement
as fortunate as the glands
bring anger flea
sordid
mine another far looting outward
sizing downward third skeletons blue
eastern bruise
carousing bruise
bracken taker hollered mountainously adores
crack to seep sight
tubular witnessing
a fragment of shade
being liquidated gaily
glacial bales furrowing nearer the claims
destined to be breed fodder
a being often gratuitous and bare to be seen

grain the bated breath
breach the oracular triumph
where
breasts come from
mice

and the lured entertain
apart from the shelves
delineate the
camembert
with a coy
toy
slow icicle slovenly
a coy a torn proboscis
afoot, mad nano director
marmalade overflowing the brassiere
flitting toward the floozy
direct
direction
directly distinct born aflame
oriflamme
bored sexual analysis togetherness floated quip
soaked thorax splitter
floorboard
all a goat
petal
priceless pedal, amorous mayor
canned product ape
mantle
alkaline alien
freakers
jut near and

garble the bra starlet afford
not nice only wince, sir, minced mice
pâté pattern edible

nor?
for knightly deem?
worth mite
digger scratch surfeit
surgery funeral
pine lady manage
manger me thorny
and I lank the prosecutor
she's a cuter hen
the hedge
a breath trapped sight of
hair
heir supplant
nor way is thicker
rye dream sack
rank and soliciting demeanors
outhouse sack
balls
crinkled fallow man
universe quiver
mime the rhombus tract
in herds hurting
veins
the desk goes forth frail
dreams bundled brown
open pouring
hen of pores distinctly posit
mice bred mistreated
all longing four
hearty door bulge up the framing mechanics of

business
isms
isthmus straight frog the under hound
untried tire marked sings the glue beep beep
bloop feel list bleeping outer knot
musicality
heaven moored
together rays clone on indefinitely piling
cone of ill nasal caprices
this frowning glob
the ephemeral udder shuddering
behind the yodeler
vastly weeps

for fruit twining plot opposite con poseur
of a reindeer shamed transgressor
to rebuke the meanings requites more conniving
than a mussel can muster
treat the winking mucus
spring of mustard
in its leotard
retarded leopard
causing an uproar
the fetters flung sky binding
no often warming hermit up a cloud steer
ornithological septum
blanket blaze crowned a fried corollary of knees
needling
hen plumping bees blown through the senior
theologian's moat

bared
reared
take that derided scalpel
and follow your undulated lemons
scraping like lemurs
burning foolish goop
not ant fur
nor moan the flask juke
a singular smile
is heard
whiskers through the trees
the withheld whisk
tints its remade bater

untitled 9

skeletal dilettantes
designate
orthodontic
neutrons
abuzz
glow of cosmic microscopes
bulbous ostrich eyes
peering
through
insecticide tubing
delineate within

Elbow Room

the self is
a little egg
and the shell
is 'I'
all that we do
within the shell
is fantasy
until we break through
the 'I'
and discover
that what was growing
on the inside
is the same as what has always been
on the outside

the immaculacy
of emptiness
space
without boundary

For Monastic Capacities
to let sing the song I love you

the cucumber's firm
and the cuckold

sweet indigestion
complaisant necessities
for the
fresh appeal
shower bowing
at the bottom
breathing

from conception to
brief river horse

a history opens in
the sun also known
ideas are off
city house
plan bride trials

the wealth man of
spring kindness
whispering
we want to see you
a work of location

bringing families Christ in hair
today
join us as we are more fun

for the dogs we talk to
creating beautiful location
what's happening
save the date
quality power of the
perfect fit
and nothing short of a
shrinking violet
members only
everything lions
in schools

change the world
at a time
at the chamber
jump into medieval garden
down venturesome spirit
beat syndrome
continues
at the orchard
for life day with the birds
center world
magical key
beautiful things with smiles
with neighbors

botanic masquerade
memories of who care
need America
permanent nature
offers a cozy gathering
mother's affiliated
and our world
now open
building upon existing
life
$1
white

make the side of prey
share the life of
white value
a gift to us all
welcomes the fine experts
on time
durable hills challenge Christ
in more sustained
fit people
your complete interior
in God's second chance
independent and private
every step of the way

little valley pulse
arrives at
free admission
enjoy man
aiming for
spectacular mustard pull
garlic trust
here are some words
local real

for the nature-word
place below deck
dental honor
trust its future rhythm

gold home
of the sparrow events
makes plans for the next century

did you know?
everything is new again
keep your sunny
cosmetic properties

building up
to strive endlessly
innovation asparagus
going for the lover
tomorrow

fight knowledge
comprehensive performance
every day of the year
always in bloom

children's
mosquito
awareness for violence
makes the man
in our community
grow

Colloquial

one bird is a
splotch on the paved way
to longer hides
slithering hold your grind
      hind legumes squirt dessert into
   marble affection infect my reel solely
   kneeling priceless garment of universal
matadors spell this fat worm two more fires
    took night by a pretty antler it was
      foretold otherwise natural
   aggregate aggressive peak after leering
blooms the frog highline a fork in the blonde
flanges angler tides be drawn into breezes
  of the mind a discarded rind my hind
laughter spoils the rimless train wheel yolks
   yuk yuk yuk kingdom righted leftovers
       today glass

A Lost Child

the balding tomato
humping its partition
and shorn of every device
angled presently
in agile agony it withstood
with intact ministry
submerged by frosted pipes
accenting a humorless terrain
hundred
hunting
underway
wheezing and trounced upon an ounce
ant bash
rotted brains
sprouted desirably
in its mortgages
and cerebral
temperaments
it is a tenor
operatic windblown
wheelbarrow
choose its feelers
gentle
the night ripples
like infinite
melons roiling down the staircase

left out in the open mound
a clever nostrum
a cleaver rises
the mists of dawn
dimmer boy
folding the meandering tails
as they cascade
hitherto unfinished
but gleaming
in the avian
gloom

my back is hunched
forward
backward
it makes no difference
the filial diffidence
is moist surrounded
bygone ear canals
the paddler lopes
grows its width
the breath
slated to burn
owl rubber

in the forest
are many tools
hidden
follow the woodpecker
like a jewel

Picking and Choosing

how easy it is
to forget
that nothing
is unendurable

every experience
is the self

heaven or hell
it's up to you

let go of them both

Windowsill

if we were
confronted
with reality
and its double
would we
know
which is the
evil one?

all that remains for us
is the mocking
laughter
reverberating down
the endless
corridor

one end is
irreducibly tiny
the other
infinitely huge

say it with me:
'all sounds are contained in the nose'
who knows
which

Sweetest Perfume

he has the sun stacked up against three
fingers, it trembles like a gong and all the
turtles release their shells into the blue-green
stars. a shape which was just a tuft of ostrich
came to light. the man suddenly split open
and turned inside out. a chicken the color of
light stood amongst the entrails. it began to
pick at his corpse. it picked and picked until a
kitchen sink was produced which had a flower
stuck in the drain. the hole curved desirably.
two girls approached riding atop a cylinder.
their shadows are vomiting but it does not
bother them, they have a scepter twisting and
turning. lines traced themselves in the sand,
painting the landscape in symbols. the girls
walked along the lines. the chicken has
devoured the inside-out man and is flushed
down the sink, the flower remains. the leg of a
beautiful ant is growing from its center. the
shadow of one of the little girls picks the ant
leg, and a frog leg grows in its place. it picks
the frog leg, and a bicycle pump grows in its
place. the other little girl steps beside the
shadow and it passes into her anus like wind.
she picks the ant leg and the frog leg from her
rear. a long winter grows in their place.

sixteen hundred horses the size of ants appear, though no one is leading them. they take away the kitchen sink. the sun places a man on the ground, he is naked and shivering. there are little asparaguses all over his body. the two little girls gather the asparaguses from him, as he coughs and coughs. a horse whinnies and a frog croaks.

it is important not to allow the arrows to stick in one's leg. the arrows hang about because of their large ovaries. no one cares to tire them. a sheath is distracted.

Unremembered

blowing into an inside-out skull will not
produce a gilded tree root, for there is no void
in which it allowably could hang suspended,
like a gamboling trigger, boiled to absolute
tension, accessible within the limber fungus,
which will have at that time communicated its
being to the raft towed by diamond bees, the
furrowing of their wings brings beads to the
perfumer's care, not to be opened until windy
reasons reply support soon the orchestration,
glooming fruitless on their artifices and
spangled pancakes. if a semblance were wont
to commune the unseeable minerals that
outcry every jewel image and numeral! the
crabs above the lake's surface deposed of
their clapping, at least inch width of ear snot.
Drainage is tumescent, as if expecting the
fairylike rousing of hinter hamlets, resin fried
undo tide. due is the moist perimeter, dewy
are the readying hints, the furiously yucking
hues, tool begone bygones dozen morass too
late at ten and freight. utmost umbrella
squeaks its platinum informing platform
shooing wayward the lesions of yeast, zipping
the careful hairless tips defrosting humming a
trough full in the oven a bagged loon belongs

midst its swoon, unswerving in a coursed
fruition steady, steady monosyllabic
frothiness besides. lame and fortune nether
waste not its ham breaded with sticky runts
and running gale the downs a prickly itched
tan lineament cast reverse thrown bologna
ball coney silo breading bed to fake zoo
primer, nonaggression in up topmost belonged
bedded long waist in the year torn come
gummy bunter. rumbling route the rails a
dumpling bloods, further scouring the
tinctured handles coming hands at humorless
dream vulvas, torqued with value, valuable
tooted a root rude rooster corks balloon form
champagne nails, turned the wind into two
peaces, pitches ruddy toggle together a glade
formal withdrawal sighting lizard out breath is
full to the peaks of lasting summits, doting the
splitting river tumble drying mountainous
affectations abound lessons relearning hurt
and doorknob snow. it would twinkle in ye
eyeless eye, the one always held by drudging
space, unsettled place of return novelty, when
did it last so long, for it to rememorialize its
patched partitions ruined winter particles it
can sell for dummy to a seeped breadth
mandate, foreclosing the terrestrial spherical
menses masturbated effortless trunk forming
up turning around handsome hand grenadier
from too many uglier battlements often

molasses drunk drowning hermit toads which forever in the future goad the mute days the wrinkle before oblivion's sandpaper rake, the future's rod is trying truth to berate healthy rascals my souls mating fragrant ahead of itself my huddling sass in cornerstone way operate isotoping helium to meager regretter. the only grappling refrigerator is laying dragons outward to dry the moored teachers trembling hundreds of barrels of feathers and unwritten latrines known from the sort of time beforehand candid atlas cast in due timely stream ruminating rampart tune blending sweating marshaling retraceable trips. usurped isn't often a fashion onto yon dressed door knave, stand astride a baleful galloped rutted out unjustified ungulate haggling fortune and windmills fleecing their own turning headlong frost. not at the fever's limpidly hurrying tried and trunk foul withered yogurt corpse hair length studded for reflection, the stead fasting studious ingratiated. tomb meals wheeled reigned inwardly gasping of trust and deserting lampoon month of brothers form a fan around the neck of a gloating gate, the hankering inside a hidden rattling turtle bone devises erratic rhapsody betide mill form or future in hiccups its itching inside outwardly tooth freshly daisy. mane of leather frowns, dromedary similarities retread titles of nothing brooks birding youthful heights are faced point down trodden by the reams forming a bandolier to sweater haven linked. the tomb loans it's riddled with erudite shards of crops ignited by feelings touched below the gestalt by gateways and undignified tufts, fig trees pigmentation all on its own alone weigh from home. home is sour of dirt, weekly leafing the absent footfalls of a commanding representation, to a manifold man, his brain upturns the membrane of a furniture goodness, withheld only onto itself attuned coarse and fertile, feral, femininity affluent bend way which is a general winding gown hold on belongs to holdings onto belongs in thirst, in hurtled, lukewarm likewise results instant instead a self-solidification magnifies callous liquidity and funeral gas moles cowering because they removed loose cysts, the remnants glibber like a pristine chapel the dowry snow fallen on angles revelatory in stare, behinds bared and freaking tulips bleed rickets at thereafter stairs too manly stared rotted root tuft after all is readily flung, glance the flangers, steadily the ruby removes its stalk to display a rose-shaped onion field the consistency of models fragrant trays beacon a hurt wait staff inflection with itself unquestionable pardoned upon a healing heaping of grief trying too hardily to belong

still ever. monstrous dilapidation if it
pleasures their firming trumpet mint, the mint
stork loading yolk per optioned potion,
proportionate to each dispassion flayed at an
athletic steak in handed yellow glow
pernicious grown dome front waters the bed
too many leapers gloaming fairly stately an
upset state huddle its governmental passage of
noxious juices luxury ripple from other plead
of trouble search the ditch forlorn truffles
untie each reverie trimmed ping snippet
young lung proceed darting mouth of every
month. work fed leech is rounded exquisitely
refrain, a draft to leaden the places collapsing
in a fitting of home longing doves working to
a delicate unison whose returning fever issues
itself thistles all boundaries are frozen
steadfastly agate agape a rapacious ape shape
on top of a horizon ready vertical, as can ever
be plainly and routinely demonstrated
upholstered worthy atmosphere of lullabies
for estimated ghouls brightly party bound
tightened ruptured nicely funnel often is rice
rapier twist. Further glint of stomached
betides, woeful dawn flowered runes
delicately cephalic return, threat evergreen to
the downs, thirty syndromes minute glance
upheld door the starriness untold folding itself
to the glare retriever, a dash, dashing it all.

Heralded

The cows have derailed the train as I enter the dromedary without ceasing. I am full of legumes and black sausages, I turn the wheel whose hub is a violet green catheter and whose spokes are chimpanzees that tremble cordially. At the center of the glamor is a plume which discourages even the most radical appetites, the whetted fields of mossy apprehension.

"Could it be the rich disappointments, the symbolic fright?" I ask of the clouds, disposable like tissues. They shriek as they sit in the air, they deposit a mirror into the open hand, the groping hand. The mandrakes answer me in secret baboons. Ephemeral lagoon. Black moss growing and transparent on the silver globe shaped like a head, jugular knucklehead glinting like a pinnacle. I am not in a room. I slip into the unseen spaces, I slip on the silver banana peel and pigeons of laughter splat overhead.

The blood on the forest speeds and
forms the words:

The pearls and the
swine
like a bunch
of grapes
dripping from the vine
further
elongated vine
into the slowly opening
turtle mouth
distinct and separate
gaping among the stars
charming instrument
that does as it pleases
to please no one
dust gathering
on the immobile golems
galvanized smile
the living breathing rabbits
swarming over
a body lying prone
like the arrow
of dawn
stuck in the guts
loosed across the table
upsetting the pot
of coffee

scalding pyramid
miracle
petunia
out float the bulbs
outpouring spangled
velocity
brother mother
        father sister

can you spare

            a dime?

But I do not have time to read them; indeed, there is the drop of a hammer bursting. Without knowing it I am shoved headlong into the butter. The goat's butter is blue and twisting like a ribbon. The horse's butter is hairy in the mud. The falcon's butter is more bitter than the falconer's butter, which exhales legs that carry it to the diseases crouched undistracted by the marbles wrenching and fizzing in the frying kettle. There is within my person a room, an average-sized room; the populations come and go as they please and I cannot see who they are behind their masks of fornication. My diametric excrement acts as a window along which fish-heads parade, their nozzles aloft, their fuel adroit. The room falls to my feet like an elevator. I walk nowhere and can smell my thoughts more clearly:

the failure of the self
to be another
self
to be something other
than the self
the failure of the self
to be
the self

is it this over which we
labor?
is this the
crime
of the self?

Between my eyes a polar bear makes love to an igloo, between my icicles the wind is swallowing porcupines by the amplitude. The running formula does not as it distresses, it becomes more fluent with each trickling errand. My attention is drawn downward to the curtains.

There he is, swimming in the vast ocean of the cosmos. He is distinguishable by the movement of his arms and legs. Flitting like a bird in and out. It is like watching a pollywog grow into a frog. The planets wink at him and breathe. I watch, I observe, pristine. Another being lopes further along. The vibrating ripples plunge into his brain, his eyes are shaped like hearts which throb like erections. She can feel his weightlessness and turns to him, she comes to a halt. He shifts ineluctably closer, closer. From a distance they entwine until they are together. They move like an immense buoy in the waves, snapping planets out of their orbits, smudging suns and moons, clapping the stars. The things in space of which humanity knows nothing, the things which exist only in imagination, yet beyond, apart from. A climax is reached, infinities are released like flatulence.

They separate slowly. In her gestation thousands of lives, thousands of deaths. He

waits, he occupies the same space thoroughly.
She remembers something. Nothing is
changed. Three eternities later it is done. A
misfire. Almost but not quite. She is beside
herself, she clips along out of sight. He
watches her go, the gloves of the deceased
fetus prickly like a quivering spine. I watch, I
observe, pristine. He passes away among the
stars. The mask of substance is removed:
emptiness wails triumphantly. But there is no
triumph, no defeat. She was crying, the tears
blossoming like flowers all over her immense
body, superficially illuminating the cosmos. It
is neither here nor there. Life is not life.

The eucalyptus is not an onion.
The feminine cote is not underneath.
The feature is not iodinated.
The quickness is not exuded.
The mechanistic framework is not diurnal.
The ululating is not gregarious.
The glandular trophy is not nauseated.

   The dismayed throat is not
   bare

rickety toothless corpse
pointed at the sun
bearing the weight of
dead sand across
the galley for
miles
across the tops of mountains
headless water
strumming the
flowers stuck in the ribcage
of a complete
surprise

the heroes are paved with mold
organic fishing
vessel
clenching hollow hilarities

the robotic flowers
which drip and buzz
allow for frequent
integration
swollen hive mouth
lung mouth

Banal Lagoon

the loom or the loam
which will it be
a tiger in your cap
a face in your cup
I hurry down the luggage
to once more
open the balloon for you
inside
the gypsy is waving hands
hands of snow
the burner that bites
the mousetrap sings 'figaro, figaro'
let us boast about it
the difference is very small
elongated
it bears the pincers of spring
like a globe

I can't stand it any longer and ruffle my glazed eyes, their vision is mute and dampened. I am not in a room. All around are silver globes which grow like human heads out of nothing. Thick black water is issued from the mouths, but only my ears are remote. The holes in my ears elope, but it does not disfigure me too plainly. If my stomach was a panther stuffed into a trumpet, if my urchin would relish the yearning urn, the firebugs glisten, the ruby excavation. Ugly depletion of the sensate senses strung along by a formidable delusion. The source of our disquiet is the lack of authenticity.

Quiet, now.

desire is such
that it does not require
fulfillment
indeed
there is no sating
desire
no relief
no release

desire tries relentlessly
to imitate time
always relinquishing
what it has obtained
time
the omnipresent threshold
through which all things pass
and none remain

for want of self
we are always in want
like spoiled children
yet
the self
is not lost
is not gained
and there is no becoming
no completion

the mind
is the most powerful drug
and we are all addicted
it fools us into believing
that these desires
that these thoughts
are our own

have we forgotten
to whom the sacrifices
are made?
what is real? what is imaginary?
who is it that enjoys gratification?

the one
on which all depend
is not there

For want of a nail...

A single mote of dust is enough to stir
the great ocean...

I do not refrain from being crushed into a fine powder; I will be scattered on the ewes like seaweed jewels. The gamblers at the next table set fire to their eyebrows; how I laughed when the horses stuck their heads out from their mouths! The old familiar scenario all over again. With my axe I remove the horse heads and heap them underneath the silver globes. The black water misinterprets this recourse and takes the shape of two thousand canary heads. My body is a thousand bodies. At this time I did not have a head of my own, there was a body in its place, a body on top of my body. But whose body? Nobody. My body a thousand bodies, my head a thousand bodies. Bobbing fraudulently. Bodies frantically.

Frankly, the thicket is not interested. To place its globe in ruddy salt or a principle wheelbarrow would do no more than ferment its cessation. So I ridiculed the esophaguses. They thumbed their noses at me, but I needed the little crowning tick to suck essences from the witnesses. Once bloated, the tick resembled the heavens, it impaled the microscope with a thermometer which had only moments before been used to pluck the strawberries growing from the penis of a sapphire wildebeest. It could have been mistaken for a chandelier, a calendar. Itching tick. There was only a slight delay.

Present Relation

The image of the sky is composed
of minuscule triangular birds
which encourages
the clock to ejaculate time
like a broken mirror
like a shattered mirror
ideal picture window
bird
symbol
I tend the nests
getting a rise
out of all the tin cans
who have lost their labels
who have put their shoes
on the wrong beak
the clock to ejaculate
the clock to emigrate
into the bathtub in the storehouse
my mouth shaped like a hippopotamus
to allow countless
tears to pass through
the unforgiving extremities
a cardboard box
into which the world was put
into which a child was put
my eyes read the word
snuff

on the inside
of my palm
I'll give it up
I'll give it to you
I'll remain in my tunnel
when I peer out
tumultuous bubbles appear
and mock these words
as I write them

When I say that the warehouse is full of white smoke, what I mean to say is that it is as immobile and solid as a huge boulder the shape of a manatee. To misinterpret is to divulge the salamander vaginas waving like totem poles in the arctic familiarity. I hesitate, but nay, to hesitate to remove to insert to disfigure graciously and with to insulate foremost and whether or not the year will bend the crab with a hundred legs is full of wine fire. If only these prophylactic stones could breathe and speak easy! The stones which comprise the funeral, the stones which are the size and color of stones. Sparkling gangling accesses. Sex is intact. Remember, remember: the failure to find meaning is a triumph. The successful meanings are greatly esteemed. Could it be that meaning is found where there is no meaning, that meaning and no-meaning are the same? The swordfish triangulates steadily, evenly, without coarseness, its flower clenches and unclenches to the ringing of a knife.

I am not in a room. What we've got here
            is a failure
      to
            communicate
      with the short
      antennae
                  protruding
      effortlessly
            from the
                  holes
      held in the hand

seek dilute drum dink bagatelle corm slip
salacious fume theologist vermin computer
                              palimpsest
monotreme organ

            self is a mirror
            not-self is a mirror
            big and
            small
            no mirror
            anywhere

      no time all the time

g

l

tttyhkl   h

uu   l

w   terw

                    dsa   j   o

        e   cvbnmn

v

    q   wdftri

u

        b

        e

        a   s   w   a   d   d   l   i   n   g

        u

khgu

            t

            i

    esw   f ul

                    d

ctcc

                e

                l

                u   rvty

    ijnhur   s

                i

            o

            n

                        s i n k
                          s i n k
     m on k e y   h o l e
s   i   n   k

                              uionm

both sexes
thrice hunkering   the daily blues
disposable   and reds
climbing stalk
                    serpent withdrawal

                    singular yeast trinity
          corporeal   testimony
utmost mosey
                        battering ram
                        ballerina dinette

      the human tank
                    human tank
     the great colostomy bag of the soul
bursting
   like the pillars of our wrath billowing
        like smoke which congeals
momentarily
                to blot out the starved sun

leaking venom like tears
which the breast of the moon
                laps eagerly
eagle

                        military tissue

                rampant depletion
                        deleterious time
circumstances   dances
                                abundant

obstructions
register trademark of the oven clouding
spittoon in the oven
                duplicate smothering

                designed to make you feel
                        privileged
                and reliable

                restricted only to the fields of
                                        vision
                        the liberating forms
                and sequined memories

the droves cry

    'liberty!'   noitcurtsed

and are fed little silver spoons
        laden with mechanical triangles

gloating

    floaters

felicitous   endgame   trombone
                d
                a
                m
                a
                 m
                e   a
                      j   j
                   a   j   a
                   j   a   j
                    a   a
                      j

The chain-sturgeon is convincingly erudite; it toots and plows among the silver globes, which I caress as if they were fumigation's teats. It is distressing to see the azure mushrooms. They sprout, they chirp like cloacae, they splinter, they refuse. I push myself into a little ball and all the silver globes attach themselves to me. I myself am attached to the stairs. Interminable. Look at my face. Looking at my face. Looting my face for the allotted penetration. Alarming sound stream. The object, the animal. Wide embraceable disaster, hiccupping with disease, there is no opportunity for advancement. No retreat, no cavalry. No illusion, no faith, no hope. Clinging clinging. Not knowing. There is a green hole in the suction print which collects the dreams of each and every one. Dreaming and crying. Like a cow containing all cows within its dilapidated hide.

The murderers and rapists have been at it for years, and probably will be for years to come. Don't be fooled: every single person is capable of anything. Depravity always shines through like a rhubarb pie at the center of a bell of chrysalises. The sane are liars; narcissism, if anything, is honest. Could it be said that everything is self-centered? Not to lose the mind is failure, yet success and failure exist only in the mind. Everyone seems so sure that tomorrow will always appear. Wherefore this confidence? Expectation is the disease of the mind. Of what can we not be certain? What do we doubt? There is no disproving anything. In some ways it is so, in some ways it is not so. The minnow symbol, buddy syndrome. Littering doesn't prove anything. Understanding is failure, because we are always mistaken; human beings produce nothing but ineptitude and falsehood. It has yet to be seen. Empty houses are we, built of bone and sealed with skin, so that none might enter in. We skulk around blindly, madly, numbed by our lucidity, we sulk and grope within our minds, searching for something else, for actuality. The absence is plainly visible. Perhaps someday we will be able to forget about violence. Nothing is spared.

A solitary heron with a herringbone bill calls out into the night's little cup. The echoes berate the smoldering intestinal formality. Mist rises from its eyes to blot out the malady. Ostrich malady outstretched. The ripples are produced by nothing, the trees strut like the shadows of a clown. Multifaceted shade, voluminous impenetrability. The bee's niece is inebriated darkly accessing worm-ridden frontiers; the levee's cheeses are indelible mandible susurration. The librarians have shed their dorsal fins and attain to glorious heights; the lamps have shed their dorsal fins. Eternity is benign, infinity is stilted. They are unpaired, unimpaired.

Charitable dolphin fingernail outside the infinitesimal forever. Identifying with everything, identifying with nothing. Flip-flop, clip-clop. I did not witness the assault, I had to turn away.

There
was   nothing
I   could
do
o o
o   o
o   o
0   0
o   o
0 o oo o 0

little EGG
independent stream

The End

To pass away
gently
like all the Ten Thousand Things
of this world
is the greatest
honor

to live
and then to not
why should it be otherwise?

     to live
     and then to not —

     thank you,
     thank you